Old Cruden Bay and Port Erro
Whinnyfold, Boddam, Buchanha
by Jim Buchan

When Whinnyfold was established in the middle of the nineteenth century, fishermen from Old Whinnyfold were among the first settlers. On the cliffs about half a mile from the old village, Whinnyfold benefited from being nearer the landing beach but it still had most of Old Whinnyfold's disadvantages. A path down the cliff face was the only access to the sloping shingle beach, suitable only for small, light craft, which had to be pulled beyond the high-water level. Whinnyfold was not on a main road and was bypassed by the Ellon to Boddam railway. The advent of steam-powered boats, competition from in-shore trawlers, and centralisation of the fishing industry in Aberdeen and Peterhead led many villagers to sell their houses, often for holiday homes, and move to a town.

Text © Jim Buchan, 2007.
First published in the United Kingdom, 2008,
by Stenlake Publishing Ltd.
Telephone: 01290 551122
www.stenlake.co.uk
ISBN 9781840334340
The publishers regret that they cannot supply
copies of any pictures featured in this book.

Acknowledgements

I wish to acknowledge the help I received when compiling this book. Members of staff in the Arbuthnot Museum and the Public Library in Peterhead, in the Grampian Transport Museum in Alford, in the Reference and Local Studies Department in Aberdeen Central Library, and in Old Aberdeen House, Aberdeen, gave invaluable assistance. I also wish to thank the staff at Aberdeenshire Heritage, Mintlaw, for their help and for permission to use the photographs on pages 35 and 50. I am also grateful for information received in conversation with Marna Cruickshank, Stanley Cordiner, Alan Middleton, Eddie Oman, Aileen and Colin Ritchie, Sandy Ritchie, and Marilyn Samways. The publishers wish to thank Margie Davidson for contributing the photographs on pages 16, 19 and 26.

Further Reading

As well as back numbers of local newspapers, the sources listed below were used by the author during his research. None is available from Stenlake Publishing.

Pollable Persons Aberdeen, 1696.
The Statistical Account of Scotland Volume XV, D.J. Withrington and I.R. Grant (eds), 1982.
The New Statistical Account of Scotland Volume XII Aberdeen, 1845.
The Third Statistical Account of Scotland Volume 7 The County of Aberdeen, 1960.
Fishing Boats And Fisher Folk On The East Coast of Scotland, Peter F. Anson, 1930.
Bram Stoker – A Biography of the Author of Dracula, Barbara Belford, 1996.
Tour To The Hebrides, James Boswell, 1785.
Bygone Buchan, Jim Buchan, 1987.

A Century of Golf at Cruden Bay, Cruden Bay Golf Club (publisher), 1998.
The Rise & Progress of the Granite Industry of Aberdeen, William Diack, 1950.
The Man Who Wrote Dracula – A Biography of Bram Stoker, Daniel Farson, 1975.
The Cruden Bay Hotel and its Tramway, Keith Jones, 2004.
Cruden and its Ministers, Adam McKay, 1912.
Banff & Buchan An Illustrated Architectural Guide, Charles McKean, 1990.
Buchan (fourth edition), John B. Pratt, 1901.
Fishing Off The Knuckle – the Fishing Villages of Buchan, David W. Summers, 1988.

INTRODUCTION

As every fisherman in early coastal villages knew, sloping sandy beaches are susceptible to breaking waves, which makes the launching and beaching of boats hazardous. Boats are liable to bed down on sand and require extra effort when being hauled above the high-water mark or relaunched. Sea towns from Whinnyfold to Buchanhaven, therefore, were usually established on cliffs or promontories with accessible shingle shores where boats could be beached safely above the high-water level.

Some etymologists have traced *Cruden* to Pictish times, while others, recalling a prehistoric stone circle which was removed from the farm of Stones by an 'improving' tenant in 1831, have derived the name from *Cro Duin* – 'the circle on the hill'. There is, however, a persistent tradition that *Cruden* signifies *'the slaughter of the Danes'*. Referring to a battle fought near the Bay of Cruden in 1012, the *Statistical Account of Scotland* (1792) says, 'In the present churchyard, which is about a mile to the westward of the place, where the old church was, there is a black marble grave stone, said to have been sent over by the Danish King, to be laid upon some of his officers, who were slain in the battle . . . . The different places, where the dead were buried, do yet strongly mark the field of the battle.'

According to another tradition, the progenitor of the ennobled Hay family came to prominence after a farmer of that name and his two sons, armed with a yoke and other farming implements, intervened in the Battle of Luncarty in Perthshire in 980. They were credited with winning a legendary Scottish victory against Danish invaders and were rewarded by the king with an estate in the Carse of Gowrie. The Hays prospered and added to their estate until King William 'the Lion' confirmed William de Hay in the barony of Erroll. In time, the Errolls began to play their part in national life. Soon after the Battle of Bannockburn in 1314, Robert the Bruce appointed Sir Gilbert Hay of Erroll as Hereditary High Constable of Scotland and gave him the barony of Slains, Aberdeenshire. Sir William Hay, fifth High Constable, was created first Earl of Erroll in 1452. From then until the twentieth earl sold Slains Castle in 1916, the Erroll family played an important part in many aspects of life in the Cruden area and an increasingly significant role in national affairs. As Lord High Constable, the eighteenth earl led a splendidly liveried retinue of mounted esquires, pages, grooms and footmen in a ceremonial parade during George IV's visit to Scotland in 1822. As Knight-Marischal of Scotland and Baron Kilmarnock of Kilmarnock, he had a seat in the House of Lords.

While on their famous journey to the Hebrides, Dr Samuel Johnson and James Boswell were shown some of Buchan's 'visitor attractions' and Sir Walter Scott highlighted one of its dramatic rock formations in *The Antiquary*. Later, in an attempt to develop the Cruden area as a holiday resort to rival Brighton, the Great North of Scotland Railway Company publicised the area's scenic and marine attractions. Shortly before the Great North of Scotland Railway's arrival, Bram Stoker visited Port Erroll and became a habitué of the area, incorporating thinly disguised local lore and settings in some of his thrillers. When Stoker opened Peterhead Flower Show in 1904, the town's provost introduced him as someone who had done much to publicise the area, especially when he had 'come to Cruden Bay before the Great North of Scotland Railway!'

Commercial quarrying of granite in the vicinity of Boddam increased rapidly in the first half of the nineteenth century as a direct result of the Industrial Revolution, which had created a huge demand for building materials for roads, bridges and harbours. Thomas Telford, for example, recommended local granite for harbour works at Peterhead in 1803. Before completing his work on London's Waterloo Bridge (built between 1811 and 1817), John Rennie was engaged to build a bridge over the Thames at Southwark and he came to Aberdeen to choose granite blocks suitable for his new contract. Quarry masters unanimously agreed that it was impossible to transport the massive blocks he had chosen and so Rennie went to Peterhead. He selected a boulder, which was manoeuvred on to a carriage, made to his specifications, and then pulled by a squad of his employees to the quayside in Peterhead. Weighing 25 tons, it was the heaviest single piece of cargo handled in Peterhead up to that time, but Rennie managed to persuade a sea captain to load it for London, where it arrived safely in spite of forebodings that it would fall through the bottom of the boat! The publicity generated by Rennie's 'big stane' – and the fact that he used Peterhead granite to build naval dockyards at Portsmouth and Sheerness – boosted the demand for top quality stone from quarries in the Peterhead area. Between 1817 and 1822, a quarry on Stirling Hill exported 213,459 dressed blocks, 75 tons of causeway blocks, and 3,890 feet for kerbs and pavements. Developments in stone polishing techniques, using steam power, gave a further boost to quarrying, which made a significant contribution to the local economy in the nineteenth century.

From the latter 1880s until the 1950s convicts from Peterhead

Prison quarried granite at Stirling Hill to build a Harbour of Refuge, a deep-water shelter from the North Sea storms, in the South Bay, Peterhead. Planned for the days when sail was still predominant, it was underused most of the time. From the early 1970s, however, with service/supply bases built inside both breakwaters, the Harbour of Refuge has played a vital role in bringing North Sea oil and gas on stream. Oil comes ashore near Whinnyfold, at the south end of the Bay of Cruden; gas at St Fergus, about five miles north of Buchanhaven. Built across Sandford Bay from Boddam, Peterhead Power Station is designed to produce electricity using gas piped from St Fergus or oil piped from a tanker jetty in the Harbour of Refuge. These developments have helped to compensate economically for the reduction of the local fishing fleet.

Above: A creel, with a spotlessly clean white band adjusted to fit the bearer's shoulders, a mutch, a freshly laundered apron, and a chequered plaid were characteristic of the fishwives who travelled the highways and byways of Buchan until well into the twentieth century. Walking distances of up to twenty miles a day to supply the regular customers on their rounds of the farming districts, fishwives bartered fish for farm produce. The opening of the Great North of Scotland Railway's line between Ellon and Boddam in 1897 allowed them to extend their sphere of operations. Creels were transported free of charge in the guards' vans and fishwives paid reduced fares.

Whinnyfold

Gathering Bait, Cruden Bay

This scene highlights the role of women in providing bait for the 'sma'lin' (small line) fishing. In earlier times the main sources of bait were indigenous mussel beds conveniently close to the various fishing villages. By the beginning of the nineteenth century, the local mussel beds were nearing exhaustion and mussels had to be imported from the Ythan estuary. This was usually done in the family fishing boat or by horse and cart. It was not uncommon, however, for mussels to be carried in creels nearly ten miles to Ward of Cruden (later Port Erroll). Once the mussels from the Ythan reached their destination, they were 'sown' on suitable areas of the local foreshore – 'scaups' – where they attached themselves to the rocks and were kept alive by the ebb and flow of the tide until required. As the railway network expanded, mussels were imported from Montrose, Findhorn, and the Cromarty Firth. To eke out the mussels, men dug for sand eels and lugworms, which buried themselves in the sandy beaches when the tide ebbed, while women and younger members of the family used old kitchen knives, with blades suitably adapted, to prise limpets from the rocks. In the last resort, mackerel and saithe, pickled during the summer as a reserve supply, were cut up and used as bait.

Photographed in Whinnyfold about 1898, members of an extended family were preparing 'sma'lins' (small lines) for the next trip to the customary inshore fishing grounds, detailed knowledge of which was passed from generation to generation. A 'sma'lin', some 50 fathoms (300 feet) long, had about 100 'sneeds' (snoods) – short lengths of string – tied to it at regular intervals. Each 'sneed' had a hook tied firmly to it by a 'tippin', homemade by fishermen by twining lengths of horsehair. The man on the left and the teenager were 'reddin' (disentangling) lines used in the previous day's fishing and checking for necessary repairs such as 'beetin' wants' – replacing missing hooks. The women had already 'sheeled' (scooped) mussels and/or limpets from their shells into the crock placed conveniently in front of the man on the right so that he could fix the bait firmly on the barbed hooks. Once baited, the 'sma'lin' was ready – weather permitting – to be 'shot' (set) on the fishing ground early next morning and hauled the following day, hopefully with a good catch of white fish.

Whinnyfold

Whinnyfold was described in the later years of the nineteenth century as a village with 'picturesque thatched cottages in a sheltered position forming the older portion (Old Whinnyfold), while perched on the very edge of the cliffs are modern dwellings (Whinnyfold) suitable for summer visitors. Whinnyfold is much favoured for picnic parties and spelding teas are a speciality' (*Spelding* – a haddock or whiting sliced open, gutted and cleaned, and dried in the open air). This view shows speldings drying on the fencing wire adjacent to the 'modern dwellings'. The woman in the picture periodically tied speldings into bundles and carried them in a creel to be sold in Peterhead, twelve miles away. The first part of the journey was often walked in the darkness of early morning and she carried a candle-lantern, which she left in the 'Plantins', the trees on the north side of Port Erroll, to be picked up on her return. Typical of a fisherman's wife, she played her part in carrying out other tasks required of members of the fishing families.

In the late sixteenth century the ninth Earl of Erroll was accused of plotting to dethrone James VI and restore Catholicism in Scotland. In 1594 he joined forces with the Earl of Huntly and defeated a royalist army at Glenlivet. Lord Erroll fled to France when the king led an army north to suppress the revolt. On reaching Aberdeen, James requisitioned '20 stane weycht' (stones weight) of powder for the 'downcasting of Slains and Strathbogie' and supervised the demolition of Erroll's castle at Old Slains. In the late 1590s, the fugitive earl made his peace with the king, returned home, and built a new Slains Castle on the edge of the cliffs at Bowness, five miles northward from the ruined tower at Old Slains. The Errolls played an increasingly important role in national affairs and, over the years, several additions were made to Slains Castle until, in 1836/37, the eighteenth earl demolished most of the 'magnificent sea-girt courtyard palace' he had inherited and, in the words of *Banff & Buchan An Illustrated Architectural Guide*, built the 'granite faced fantasy-Baronial confection' featured here.

En route to the Western Isles in 1773, Dr Samuel Johnson and James Boswell were honoured guests in Slains Castle. Dr Johnson said the castle was 'built upon the margin of the sea so that the walls of one of the towers seem only a continuation of the rock, the foot of which is beaten by the waves'. Boswell's *Journal* records that he was kept awake by the blazing fire in his room, the roaring of the sea, and 'the pillows made of feathers of some sea-fowl, which had to me a disagréeable smell'. He also said that a previous earl had added a gallery around the inner courtyard. It was 'built of brick, both on the first and second storey, the house being no higher, so that he always has a dry walk; and the rooms, to which formerly there was no approach but through each other, now have all separate entries from the gallery, which is hung with Hogarth prints and other works'. This was the last significant alteration before the reconstruction of 1836/37.

The nineteenth Earl of Erroll was accompanied by his wife while he served as a major in the Rifle Brigade during the Crimean War; in Constantinople she was presented with a white horse by the sultan! Home again after being wounded in the Battle of the Alma, the earl banned a workhouse on his estate but supplied food and clothing for paupers. Rents of £2 to £3 annually were about half the county average and widows had free security of tenure. He provided a reading room and other recreational facilities and helped to build a harbour, a school, and a Congregational church in Port Erroll. Due mainly to his largesse, estate duties after his death in 1891, and increased taxation in the early years of the twentieth century, his successor had to sell the Erroll estate in 1916. The new owner, shipping magnate John Ellerman, was an absentee landlord who rented Slains Castle during the summer months to celebrities including Prime Minister Herbert Asquith. Ellerman disposed of the castle in 1923 to Londoner Percy Harvey who lodged a caretaker and his family in the castle until its roof was removed in 1925. Joists, windows, doors, flooring, sarking, bathroom fittings, 1,000 tons of dressed granite and 'other splendid building material, cheap for immediate delivery' from Slains Castle were advertised in the *Buchan Observer* on 5 January 1926. Since then, the castle has remained a hollow shell.

Slains Castle

During their visit to Slains Castle in 1773, Dr Johnson and James Boswell were shown some of the dramatic rock formations in the vicinity. Describing Dunbuy Rock in his inimitable way, Johnson wrote, 'Dunbuy, in Erse (Gaelic), said to signify the *Yellow Rock*, is a double protuberance of stone, open to the main sea on one side, and parted from the land by a very narrow channel [not shown in this photograph] on the other. It has its name and its colour from the dung of innumerable sea-fowls, which, in spring, choose this place as convenient for incubation.' Dunbuy became more widely known when Sir Walter Scott featured it in *The Antiquary* (1816). 'The best craigsman (rock climber) that ever speel'd heugh [climbed a crag]' he wrote, 'broke his neck on the Dunbuy.'

Below: *Pollable Persons Aberdeen 1696* recorded twenty-one residents in the fishing village of Bullers Buchan (later known as Bullers o' Buchan). Eight 'whytfishers' and their families accounted for seventeen of them; the other four inhabitants were identified as a seaman and his houshold. In spite of the disadvantages of its location, graphically illustrated here, Bullers o' Buchan functioned as a fishing village for some two hundred years. Changes in the local herring fishery, however, and the decline of line fishing in the 1890s, meant that by the end of the nineteenth century only six fishermen lived in the village which had been largely taken over by quarry workers. The Great North of Scotland Railway's branch line from Ellon to Boddam (1897) had a platform halt at Bullers o' Buchan, but this was more for the convenience of visitors to the Pot of Buller's o' Buchan than for the benefit of the fishing fraternity. During the twentieth century Bullers o' Buchan became progressively a village of holiday homes.

Above: According to the *Statistical Account of Scotland* (1792), 'The Pot of Buller's Buchan is so well known that a description would be superfluous.' When Dr Johnson and Boswell visited Bullers o' Buchan they walked round the Pot and then sailed into it. Boswell wrote in his *Journal*, 'On the quarter to the sea, there is a high arch in the rock, which the force of the tempest has driven out. In some places the rock is very narrow, and on each side you have a sea deep enough for a man-of-war to ride in, so that it is somewhat horrid to move along. The entry is so narrow that oars cannot be used; the method of entry is to row very hard when you come near it, and give the boat such a rapidity of motion that she glides in.' Their guide said that visitors to the mineral spring at Peterhead 'made parties and dined in one of the caves here'. He also explained that a strong east wind caused the sea to surge through the archway, giving the Pot the appearance of a large boiling cauldron, hence the name 'Buller', derived from the French *bouillir* – to boil.

Kilmarnock Arms, Cruden Bay.

When the Countess of Erroll died in 1758, her great-nephew, Lord Boyd, changed his name to Hay and succeeded her as the fifteenth Earl of Erroll. According to a publicity leaflet, the Kilmarnock Arms Hotel was named after the fifteenth earl's father, the Jacobite fourth Earl of Kilmarnock, who was beheaded at the Tower of London in 1746. Bram Stoker visited Peterhead for a holiday in August 1893, after friends recommended the area's bracing air. During one of his coastal walks, he 'discovered' Port Erroll with its 'one small hotel [the Kilmarnock Arms], down on the western bank of the Water of Cruden, with a fringe of willows protecting its sunken garden full of fruits and flowers'. He checked in for the remainder of his holiday. Fascinated by the lore and superstitions of the district, Stoker began to write the first of his 'Cruden inspired' books, *The Watter's Mou'*, before he returned to London. He visited the Cruden area frequently during the next seventeen years, staying in the Kilmarnock Arms Hotel (while his dog was kennelled in a nearby house) or in cottages in Port Erroll or Whinnyfold.

Old Barley Mill, near Slains Castle.

29175

Stoker returned to the Kilmarnock Arms Hotel in 1894 and finished the story which he had begun on his previous visit. He was well acquainted with the old barley mill and the area between it and a nearby inlet known locally as the 'Aal Watter Mou' (Old Water Mouth) – hence the title, *The Watter's Mou'*. Stoker was also familiar with Port Erroll's 'little coastguard lookout beside a tall flagstaff on the northern cliff', where he stationed Sailor Willy, the hero of the tragic love story. Port Erroll was confirmed as the setting of the book when one of the characters said, ''Saw Bella Cruickshank hand ye the telegram as ye went by the Post Office'.' Mrs Cruickshank was the young postmistress in the Postal and Telegraph Office, accommodated in the Kilmarnock Arms Hotel at the time. One of Stoker's biographers interviewed the nonagenarian Mrs Cruickshank, who said that Bram and his wife, Florence (known locally as Mrs Bram) often walked to Whinnyfold and 'waved to her as they passed'. She also revealed that Stoker did not play golf but Mrs Bram did.

Kilmarnock Hotel and the Bridge, Cruden Bay.

Stoker visited Port Erroll again in 1895 and wrote several chapters of *Dracula*, which, according to some literary critics, shows definite signs of being associated with the neighbourhood of Slains Castle. After *Dracula* was published in 1897, the Stoker family revisited Port Erroll. He had heard that the nineteenth Earl of Erroll, who died in 1891, liked to walk about the village 'in a tweed suit of antique cut and wearing a high Glengarry bonnet with a falcon crest'. This gave Stoker the idea for a story and he wrote *Crooken Sands* (alias the Bay of Cruden) about an eccentric London merchant, who dressed as a Highland chieftain with claymore, dirk, and pistols while on holiday in Port Erroll. The Kilmarnock Arms Hotel, with 'Sitting Rooms, Dining Hall, 12 bedrooms and 2 bathrooms (hot and cold water)', was advertised at the time as 'conveniently based for the new Cruden Railway'. In 1900 Stoker featured the Kilmarnock Arms Hotel and the nearby bridge in *The Mystery of the Seas* (the bridge in Stoker's story was replaced in 1908/09).

Some of the inhabitants of Whinnyfold gathering driftwood on the shore near the village. In summer, the area was very susceptible to haar; in winter, winds from the southeast whipped up violent storms lasting for days. As a result the Scaurs of Cruden, a reef about a mile offshore, became notorious for shipwrecks. Much of the wood, obviously tooled, probably came from the wreckage of a boat which had foundered on the Scaurs. There was no lifeboat stationed near the village but the fishermen of Whinnyfold gained a legendary reputation for going to the aid of stranded vessels. According to local superstition, when there was a full moon at the Lammas tide (1 August) people with 'the sight' could see the blanched bodies of seamen, who had drowned on the Scaurs in the past year, come out of the sea and proceed to St Olave's Well so that they could join their spirits in heaven or hell. Bram Stoker recycled the superstition in *The Mystery of the Seas* when he lodged his hero in the Kilmarnock Arms Hotel and gave him 'the sight' for the first time at the nearby bridge.

Whinnyfold

Travelling via Dyce and Ellon to a junction at Maud, the Formartine & Buchan Railway linked Aberdeen with Peterhead in 1862, and with Fraserburgh in 1865. From 1866, when they were taken over by the Great North of Scotland Railway, those lines were known as the Buchan Section. Some thirty years later Ellon Station was altered to serve as a junction linking the existing network with a new line, the Cruden Section, running as far as Boddam. Two special trains conveyed between 500 and 600 guests from Aberdeen while passengers in horse-drawn vehicles came from Slains Castle to see the Countess of Erroll cut the first sod in the project. Intermediate stations were built at Auchmacoy, Pitlurg, Hatton, Cruden Bay (also known as Port Erroll), and Longhaven. There was a platform halt at Bullers o' Buchan and sidings were provided later for granite quarries at Blackhills and Longhaven and for the Cruden brick and tile works. The first passenger train from Boddam to Ellon – a 'special' for members of two friendly societies, the Rocksley Lodge of Free Gardeners and the Buchanness Lodge of Oddfellows – ran on 31 July 1897. Scheduled services began two days later. The minister in Cruden Parish Church welcomed the railway with a sermon on *Isaiah* Chapter XXXV, Verse 8, which begins 'And an highway shall be there'!

The Great North of Scotland Railway Board acquired the Palace Hotel in Aberdeen (bottom right in the montage) and, after modernisation, reopened it in August 1891. Spurred on by its success, and with the Cruden branch line under construction, the Board began to plan a hotel at Port Erroll. Advance publicity said that, three floors high, it was in the 'Scotch baronial style of architecture' with a battlemented and turreted eighty-four-feet high square tower above the doorway. It was planned with ninety-four bedrooms, bathrooms and other conveniences, passenger and luggage lifts, electric lighting, and elegantly appointed 'large coffee and breakfast rooms and drawing, reading, and writing rooms'. The hotel (central in the montage) was expected to be ready for visitors by May 1898 and the GNSR Board was confident that, with 'the natural beauty of the surroundings and its three miles of golf course', it would 'rank with the finest establishments of the kind in Scotland'.

Photographed probably between 1910 and 1912, when Slains Castle and Cruden Bay Hotel were visited by the rich and famous, chauffeur-driven cars such as this were seen frequently in Port Erroll. At that time many of the vehicles carried a *stephany rim*, a spokeless wheel which could be bolted to a wheel for temporary use if its tyre became unserviceable. If this had to be done in darkness the driver used a detachable gas lamp fitted in front of the radiator and fuelled by a gas generator carried on a running board. Several aficianados of veteran cars have been unable to identify this model: apparently the cover for petrol and oil tanks between the windscreen and the engine cowling is an unusual shape. Eider down quilts, bogie roll tobacco, cycles and 'Furs Cleaned Dyed Made Up & ReLined' featured in the incongruous range of goods and services provided by A. & J. Milne in the shop and the garage behind. The Edgar family acquired the business in 1938 and carried on the shop along with the garage and petrol pumps behind it. The latter were moved to the site of the Aulton Garage in 1947 but the shop housing the Cruden Bay Post Office since 1961 and with *EDGAR* above the door, remains on its original site on Main Street in the village.

Costing about £22,000, nearly a year behind schedule but destined to be the flagship of the Great North Of Scotland Railway hotels, Cruden Bay Hotel was opened on 1 March 1899 with the declared objective of fostering tourism and making Port Erroll the 'Brighton of Aberdeenshire'. The local press reported, 'The weather, for a March day, was delightfully fine and gave a pleasant foretaste of how charming a holiday will be at this new resort. The hotel, with its finely dressed masonry, of delicate pink hue, stood out a handsome pile in the light of the brilliant day. A pleasant breeze bore on its wings a delicious and invigorating whiff of ozone. In the foreground lay the golf links, a fine stretch of sandy dunes, abounding in hazards calculated to test the most experienced golfer in every department of the game.' Within six months of opening, the hotel took delivery of a purpose-built, inshore rescue boat, made of larch and fitted with airtight compartments, 'the latest addition to the amenities of what is proving a popular golfing and bathing resort'.

According to one source, the original Port Erroll golf course was in use until 1895 when Cruden Bay Station and the new railway to Boddam 'cut off half of the course'. Some four years later, the *Buchan Observer* described Cruden Bay Hotel's main attraction as the eighteen-hole course designed by Tom Morris of St Andrews, aided by Archie Simpson of Balgownie, Aberdeen. On 21 April 1899, *GOLF Magazine* commented, 'Never was a Links more adapted by nature for a golf course than that fine stretch of ground lying round the Bay of Cruden'. This judgement was confirmed by the senior judge of the Court of Session in Scotland, the Lord Advocate, who pronounced the course to be potentially one of the best in the country! Golfers were offered cheap fares on the railway and cyclists were informed that there was a hall available for storing cycles. The Pavilion, now a listed building, is a lasting reminder of the halcyon days of the Great North of Scotland Railway and its luxury hotel.

The Great North of Scotland Railway Board promoted an inaugural 'Open Professional Tournament' at Cruden Bay, on 14 and 15 April 1899, with prize money amounting to £120. Visitors were advised to apply early to the manager if they wished to stay in the hotel and were informed that 'a Marquee will be erected adjoining the Golf Course at which Luncheons, Teas, and other refreshments can be obtained at Moderate Charges'. Harry Vardon, the only man to win the British Open Championship six times, won £30 with a score of 162 for the two rounds; J. Kinnell, Prestwick, won £20 with a score of 163; and A. Simpson, Aberdeen, who had helped to design the course, won £12 with 164. The press report continued, 'It only remains to be said that all the visitors to Cruden Bay were delighted with the place. Nothing but admiration was expressed for the comforts afforded at the hotel, for the bracing nature of the air of the Bay, for the picturesqueness [sic] of the scenery, and for the excellence of the golf course, the professionals being particularly delighted with the sporting character of the links.'

By 1909 the Cruden Bay Professional Tournament was firmly established on the annual professional calendar. The telegraph office, situated in the Kilmarnock Arms Hotel, required special staff to handle the extra workload during the tournament. There was a record crowd on the Saturday afternoon, when well over 1,500 spectators saw 'the old firm' more than hold their own against 'the younger school'. As the paper said, Taylor, Braid, Harry Vardon, and Herd 'took away with them no less than £79 of the £148 in prize-money'. Reporting that Taylor beat Braid in the final, the paper rejoiced in announcing that the winner used a ball named 'Colonel' and made in Scotland! It also was glad to say that 'all the professionals left Cruden Bay deeply impressed with the beauty of the district and the excellence of the course. Glorious weather prevailed and the southern golfers had no need for the extra clothing or the red balls they were advised to take with them in case they should be caught in a snowstorm!'

The Great North of Scotland Railway's advertisements for the Cruden Bay Hotel continued to emphasise the top quality golf course, the bracing air, the sandy beach at the Bay of Cruden, sea bathing, boating, fishing, splendid rock scenery, bowling greens, tennis courts, croquet lawns, and 'every modern accommodation for comfort'. Prime Ministers Lloyd George and Asquith visited the hotel and tycoons including Burrell (shipping), Coats (thread), Colman (mustard), Crawford (biscuits), Gilbey (port wine), McEwan (beer), and Wills (cigarettes), were 'kent faces'. The hotel prospered in its early years but was scarcely profitable after 1909. It was kept open, however, even when passenger services were withdrawn from the Cruden Section of the railway in 1932. The railway board arranged motor transport for guests, on a seasonal basis, between Aberdeen Joint Station and the Cruden Bay Hotel until it was requisitioned by the Ministry of War on 2 September 1939. From August 1940 to May 1941 squads of recruits from the Gordon Highlanders' depot in Aberdeen were billeted in the hotel for a month's field training under the command of Lord Aberdeen. After the hotel was de-requisitioned in 1945, attempts were made to dispose of it for conversion for other uses, before it was sold in 1947 to a Glasgow firm for demolition. Doors, fittings, flooring, and panelling were recycled and some of the dressed granite was used in building Brotherton House, Johnshaven, and council-owned flats in Peterhead.

LENDRUM TERRACE NEAR STIRLING VILLAGE

Posted in Boddam on 6 July 1908, this card of Lendrum Terrace, near Stirling Village, informed a gentleman in Streatham, London, that the sender was 'very sorry to say that I cannot caddy for you as I have commenced work'. The sender would have qualified to caddy at Cruden Bay when he passed the requisite examination after attending classes run by the course professional. A golfer wishing to engage a caddy paid a shilling (twelve pence) to the caddy-master for a caddy ticket. At the end of a round, the golfer gave the ticket to the caddy, who returned it to the caddy-master in exchange for nine pence. Some regular visitors, for example the 'gentleman from Streatham', tried to book their favourite caddies in advance of their visit. Some, Sir Jeremiah Coleman for example, paid above the standard rate. At the end of Coleman's holiday his caddy received a sovereign (twenty shillings) and a kiss from Lady Coleman! Although the halcyon days of the local quarries had by then passed, of the seventeen workmen residing in Lendrum Terrace, fourteen – including the father of the erstwhile caddy – worked in some capacity in the granite industry.

During the nineteenth century new ways of threshing grain gradually replaced the flail. Threshing mills were driven by big water wheels on some farms where there was a supply of water from a river or stream; elsewhere, mills were driven by wheels turned by horses walking round in a circle. Threshing mills driven by steam engines were built in the steadings on some of the big farms. (They went out of fashion because of the dangers posed by rusting boilers.) However, most of the tenant farmers used flails until they could hire a mobile 'thrashin' mull' from an agricultural contractor for an annual 'big thrash' of the season's harvest. The mill, with an engine to drive it, was pulled by horses from farm to farm until it was replaced by a mill pulled and driven by a steam traction engine. Based at Longhaven Smiddy this engine was photographed at Hill of Gask Farm near Cruden Bay. The threshing mill is not shown here but the top of the flywheel for the belt to drive it is visible on the far side. This photograph appeared on a postcard postmarked in Hatton in 1909.

In June 1899 the Great North of Scotland Railway Board introduced a 3 ft 6? in. gauge tramway between Cruden Bay Hotel and Cruden Bay Station, over half a mile away. Hotel residents travelled free; others paid threepence. Two tramcars, powered via overhead wires by locally generated electricity, and specially designed rolling stock (van, trailer for carrying coal, and two bogies for heavy goods) were built in the Great North of Scotland Railway's works at Kittybrewster, Aberdeen. With sixteen upholstered seats in a passenger compartment, each tram had a gated platform area for luggage and laundry baskets; laundry from all the GNSR hotels was processed at the Cruden Bay Hotel. After the disastrous fire at Cruden Bay Station in 1931 and the withdrawal of passenger services from the Cruden Section of the railway in 1932, goods trains still ran to Boddam. The tramway remained operational until 1941 when the permanent way was lifted to become scrap metal for the war effort. In 1987 one of the trams, used as a summerhouse in Hatton, was moved to Aberdeen to be restored. It was transferred to the Grampian Transport Museum, Alford, Aberdeenshire, and exhibited as an ongoing restoration project for four years before being completely refurbished in Glasgow by specialist engineers. In its original GNSR livery – purple lake, green and white – it returned to the museum in October 2000. The GNSR became part of the London & North Eastern Railway in 1923; the trams shown in this picture are in standard teak livery of the LNER livery.

As well as building the tramway, the Great North of Scotland Railway Board, anticipating the superior class of clientele which they hoped to attract to the nearby hotel and golf course, decided to add a few 'extras' to Cruden Bay Station. First and second-class waiting rooms and a refreshment room were provided and both platforms were covered with glass canopies. The station was undergoing a face-lift in readiness for the holiday season when, on 23 April 1931, a painter with a blowtorch accidentally set fire to the main building on the 'up' line. Although there was a nearby stream, there were no adequate fire-fighting appliances and the members of staff were more or less helpless. Fire brigades were summoned from Peterhead and Aberdeen and they managed to save the waiting room on the 'down' platform, the signal box, and the wooden overhead bridge.

The Cruden branch line had never been a money-spinner and the London & North Eastern Railway board decided not to rebuild the fire-ravaged station. Instead, they took the opportunity to downgrade it and removed the passing loop and the signalling apparatus. As shown on the left of this card, the building on the 'down' platform became the station office, with an old coach body as a store. The van in the centre of the photograph was part of the rolling stock for the tramway, which remained operational after passenger services were withdrawn from the Ellon to Boddam line in 1932. The tramcars continued to transport laundry from other LNER hotels as well as coal from the branch line station to Cruden Bay Hotel. In 1934 the LNER provided a large Rolls Royce limousine to convey guests for Cruden Bay Hotel from Aberdeen Station.

A Port Erroll fisherman, with a plateful of bait on his knee, preparing a 'sma'lin' for his next trip. With the baited hooks placed in such a way as to minimise the possibility of their becoming entangled when being 'shot' (set), the line was coiled carefully into a shallow wicker basket, known locally as a 'scull', ready to be carried to the boat. As illustrated in this book, in Whinnyfold and Buchanhaven 'sma'lins' were baited in the open air, weather permitting.

Port Erroll/ Cruden Bay

The Statistical Account of Scotland (1792) suggested that 'a very safe landing place for boats or larger vessels' could be made by diverting the Water of Cruden to enter the sea 'at the end of the beach next the Ward', i.e. at the northern end of the Bay of Cruden. The Water of Cruden was diverted in 1798 and the Earl of Erroll planned a new fishing village – Ward of Cruden – at the foot of the Ward Hill. The old village on the headland was abandoned and families came from other fishing villages to settle in Ward of Cruden. With the local peat mosses 'fast wearing away', the harbour was inadequate for importing a year-round supply of coal. Eventually, a Board of Trade Order in the 1870s authorised the nineteenth Earl of Erroll to build another harbour. By 1880 two basins – an outer and an inner – were completed and Ward of Cruden was renamed Port Erroll. This photograph, looking northward across the inner basin to the Ward Hill, was probably taken in the 1890s.

This view looking south across the inner basin of Port Erroll harbour shows boats drawn up beyond the slipway at the top-right corner and the Bay of Cruden in the background. Part of the slipway for the Royal National Lifeboat Institute boathouse is visible in the bottom-right corner. When necessary, the booms lying near the manually operated crane were used to close the entrance to the basin to reduce silting by water-borne sand and to give extra protection to boats. The tidal harbour, with limited space on the quays, was not equipped for steam drifters and was eventually used mainly by yawls. When Sir John Ellerman sold the Erroll estate in 1923, he offered the harbour and £250 to the village fishermen on condition that they raised £250 to add to a Scottish Fisheries Board grant of £500 for harbour maintenance. On Saturday, 24 March 1923 over £200 was raised at a sale of work for the Port Erroll Harbour Fund, 'with a view to the harbour being taken over by the fishermen' and the outstanding balance was raised. Managed by a local committee, the harbour is currently used by a few small boats catching white fish, shellfish and salmon.

The Royal National Lifeboat Institution (RNLI) stationed a lifeboat, the thirty-three feet long *Peep o' Day*, at Ward of Cruden in 1876 when the new harbour was under construction. The boathouse was erected in 1878 at a cost of £510 and the slipway, costing £70, came into service in 1879. The *Peep o' Day* was called out five times and rescued three people before being replaced in 1888 by the thirty-four feet *Frances Camilla Howard*, which cost £376. After twelve rescue missions, in which thirty-three people were saved, she was replaced in 1904 by the thirty-eight feet *John Fortune*, the last lifeboat to be stationed at Port Erroll. Costing £1,007, she is pictured here on the launching cradle outside the boathouse at the top of the slipway. Due largely to the centralisation of the fishing industry in Peterhead and the resultant migration of fishermen from Port Erroll, it became increasingly difficult to form a crew for the lifeboat. The lifeboat station was closed in 1914 but reopened the following year after arrangements were made to transport a crew from Peterhead when required. However, it closed permanently in 1921.

Tempion Rock on the Cruden Coast.
Where the Wislow Hall was wrecked, January, 1912.

The *Wistow Hall* (the name printed on the photograph's caption is incorrect), a 3,314-ton steamer sailing from Jarrow to Glasgow, was hit by huge waves when off the Longstone Lighthouse on 16 January 1912. Masts and funnels were washed away, boiler fires extinguished, holds flooded, and some of the crew, including the captain, injured. Two days later the steamer was sighted firing distress signals and drifting helplessly northward off Port Erroll. The storm prevented the launch of the RNLI lifeboat at Port Erroll and so the local Life Saving Apparatus (LSA) Company was mustered. LSA companies, comprising volunteers and professional coastguards, when available, were stationed at suitable sites on the coast. Each LSA unit had a purpose-built cart, which carried rocket-launching apparatus and a breeches buoy. Pulled manually or by horses, the rocket launching apparatus came into its own if a vessel grounded inshore, out of reach of a lifeboat. When a rocket with a line attached was fired across a stricken vessel and its crew retrieved the line, it was possible to use the breeches buoy to rescue them one at a time. Port Erroll LSA Company tracked the *Wistow Hall* past Slains Castle, where windows were damaged by waves breaking over the building. The vessel hit the Tempion Rock at North Haven and sank before the rocket apparatus could be used. The captain and three lascars – Indians employed as stokers – survived. The remainder of the crew, fifteen British nationals and thirty-eight foreigners, perished in the worst shipping disaster on the Buchan coast.

The first brickworks in the Cruden area was established in 1879, near the site later occupied by the Aulton Garage. This photograph was taken in 1880 by John Smith, a local tailor and part-time photographer. The brickworks was abandoned in 1881 due to problems caused by blown sand, but the house intended for the works manager, partially built in the picture, was completed and in due course became the property of the garage owner. St Olaf's Hotel now stands adjacent to the site of another brickworks, which was built in 1882 but ceased production in 1902. The Cruden Bay Brick and Tile Company then established the third and last local brickworks on the northern outskirts of the village. It was powered by a 1905 Marshall steam engine, generating 100hp. The exhaust from the engine was channelled under the driers to hasten the finishing process for the bricks, tiles and pipes. There were casualties among the staff when the works was bombed by the Luftwaffe in 1941. Production was restored and continued until the 1980s.

On 20 June 1914 a Norwegian named Tryggve Gran, who had flown the English Channel, was reported to be planning to attempt the first flight across the North Sea. In 1910 he had accepted Captain Scott's invitation to join the crew of the *Terra Nova* on an expedition to the South Pole and was in the search party which found the bodies of Scott and his companions, who died after reaching the Pole in 1912. Gran climbed Mount Erebus, an active volcano (13,120 feet) on Ross Island, Antarctica, before the *Terra Nova* sailed for England via New Zealand, where he climbed Mount Cook (12,350 feet). A born adventurer, he qualified as a pilot in 1914 and honed his flying skills with Bleriot, the French aviation pioneer, who sold him a plane at half price for his North Sea flight. Named *Ca Flotte*, with an 80hp engine, it was transported in sections to Port Erroll, where it was assembled on 17 July. Gran announced that he would make for Stavanger as soon as 'a day comes when the weather looks fair and settled'. Still grounded on 24 July, he had to remove the plane's wings and increase the number of guy ropes anchoring the fuselage to prevent it being blown away!

With war in Europe imminent, an embargo was placed on civilian aircraft flying from Britain after 6 p.m. on 30 July 1914. At 6 a.m. on 30 July a cablegram from Norway reported suitable flying conditions! As Gran prepared for take off, he said, 'I shall not trouble much about a map. I shall have just a piece of the Norwegian coast in front of me.' *Ca Flotte* had air cushions fitted in the fuselage; Gran explained, 'There are many steamship routes, so if I drop on the way I shall have a very good chance of being picked up within a few hours.' Airborne soon after 8 a.m., he headed for Norway, but he was forced to return when dense fog made it difficult to see the compass in the open cockpit and was back on Cruden Bay beach by 9 a.m. A girl fixed a Scottish thistle on the plane and the famous singer, Clara Butt, a guest in Slains Castle at the time, wished him godspeed before he took off again. In spite of fog and head winds, airsickness, trouble with an emergency fuel tank, and a momentary engine failure, he eventually reached the beach near Stavanger. With fuel for less than another thirty minutes' flying, he had flown 305 miles in four hours and ten minutes. Monuments at Stavanger and Cruden Bay commemorate his flight, which the *Peterhead Sentinel* described under the headline 'Gran did gran'.

LADIES BRIDGE, CRUDEN BAY.

In January 1916 a ferocious wind wrought havoc on the Buchan coast and the wooden bridge across the Cruden Burn at Port Erroll was completely destroyed. Years passed before action was taken to replace the bridge. Early in March 1922 a committee of ex-servicemen organised a fancy dress dance in aid of the Footbridge Fund. A week later the *Buchan Observer* reported, 'The Port Erroll Footbridge Committee is now active in the matter of a handsome new bridge and plans to replace the one blown down by the heavy gale early in 1916 have been approved. A considerable sum is in the hands of the committee and with a view to the complete amount necessary to carry out the scheme, they recently sent out a call to the ladies for assistance.' Within a fortnight the ladies organised a sale of work which raised over £180, 'making the building of a new bridge financially possible'. Opened on Saturday, 27 January 1923, it was named Ladies' Bridge.

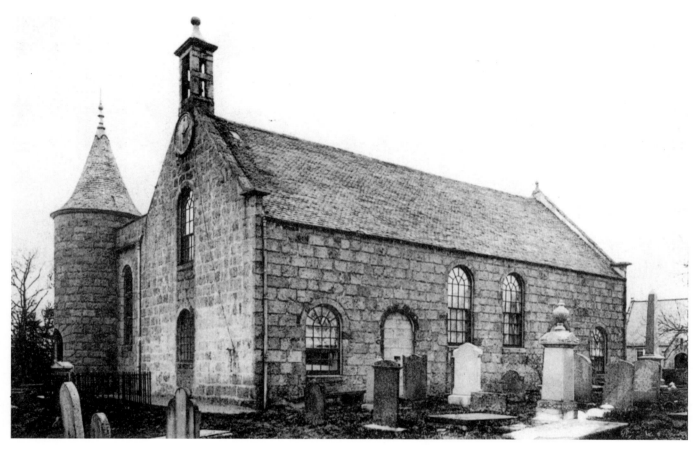

After his victory over the Danes in 1012, Malcolm II is said to have built the first church in Cruden, dedicated to St Olaf, to mark the place where the slain were buried and to commemorate the treaty of lasting peace between the combatants. This church and its successor were overblown by sand. A third church, erected in the sixteenth century on the site now occupied by Cruden Parish Church, was demolished in 1776. The outer walls of its replacement, on the same site, were built from one boulder, the Grey Stone of Ardendraught, taken from Aulton farm. The congregation worshipped in the open air until the building was finished; on the first Sunday in the new church, the minister preached on the text, 'How amiable are thy tabernacles, O' Lord of Hosts'! In 1833 the north wall of the church was removed, a new wing built, and two identical, conically roofed towers added to give access to the gallery. According to *Banff & Buchan An Illustrated Architectural Guide*, 'an otherwise standard granite box kirk, with customary birdcage bellcote topping the west gable' was transformed into 'a fantasy'.

John Burnett Pratt, born in 1798 at Slacks of Cairnbanno, Aberdeenshire, was a pupil at New Deer parish school. In 1820 he graduated MA at King's College, Aberdeen, and five years later became the incumbent of St James's Scotch Episcopal Chapel, Cruden, where he died, in harness, in 1869. Due to his initiative, a new church, financed mainly by public subscription, was erected in 1843. Designed in the Early English style by William Hay, a Peterhead grain merchant's son who studied architecture while convalescing from a leg break, its tall tower became a landmark for seafarers. Hay later designed the Music Hall and the Free South Church in Peterhead, St John's Episcopal Church in Longside, and buildings in Nova Scotia, Newfoundland, Toronto, and Bermuda. Pratt, an honorary LLD of Aberdeen University, published a series of theological works and also wrote on secular topics. His topographical masterpiece, *Buchan*, published in 1858 and reproduced as a fourth (updated) edition in 1901, is now a prized collectors' item.

After years of conflict regarding the appointment of ministers and the extent of political and judicial control, in 1843 the Moderator and over 400 ministers walked out of the General Assembly of the Church of Scotland and formed the Free Church of Scotland. The 'Disruption' followed when 470 ministers, accompanied by members of their congregations, seceded, leaving their churches to worship elsewhere. The Rev. Alexander Philip and about half of the congregation at Hatton of Cruden were among the seceders. Their first service was held in a barn at the farm of Stones. In the following week, a wooden church was built at the Mill of Hatton and was used until a stone church was erected later in the same year. The foundation stone of its replacement was laid in 1884, after the minister raised the first £1,000 towards its cost. The balance was met by means of a bazaar in August 1885 and the new United Free church was opened in the same month. Ten years later a clock and a bell were installed in the building, which is now Cruden West Parish Church.

None of the three churches described earlier were sited conveniently for the residents in the Ward of Cruden. In an attempt to cater for them and other non-adherents in the parish, the Ward Meeting House was built in the early 1870s, 'for use by all evangelical ministers'. Many villagers were still not satisfied and, at a public meeting in December 1882, it was decided to form a Congregational church. Two years later, with help from the nineteenth Earl of Erroll, a church with seating for 450 people was built near the seaward end of Main Street, Port Erroll (previously named Ward of Cruden). As reported in *Cruden and its Ministers* instrumental music was introduced in the early 1890s as 'a useful and attractive addition to the service'. Some twenty years later 'a heating and lighting installation by means of petrol gas was introduced', and a Sunday school, a work party, and a Band of Hope organised. As a result of the continuing centralisation of the fishing industry in Aberdeen and Peterhead many of the fisher families migrated from the village, causing a significant decline in the congregation. A report dated 1951 in the *Third Statistical Account of Scotland* commented that 'though its [the Congregational Church] communicant membership was small, it has a considerable number of adherents among the fishing community'. There has been a decline in the congregation since then, but, though the preacher may vary from week to week, the church bell still rings on Sunday.

Before the coming of the Great North of Scotland Railway branch line to Boddam, a granite quarry was worked in the area in the left foreground, around the bridge carrying the permanent way as it neared its terminus. The lighthouse stands on the rocky islet known as the Yards of Boddam, while to the right Buchan Ness Lodge is perched on the edge of a cliff. Across the gorge from the lodge, on the extreme right, stand the ruins of Boddam Castle, apparently built in the sixteenth century and occupied until the early years of the eighteenth century. In *Banff and Buchan An Illustrated Architectural Guide*, Charles McKean writes, 'this seat of the Keiths of Lundquharn, on an impressive cliff-girt peninsula, probably comprised a tower in the corner of an impressive courtyard of outbuildings including a chapel'. There is no record of a drawbridge but some large hinges, usable for such a feature, were discovered in a trench being dug near the entrance to the castle in 1868.

BUCHAN NESS LODGE, BODDAM

Pratt's *Buchan* refers to Buchan Ness Lodge as 'Lord Aberdeen's Marine Villa'. 'Walks have been cut along the face of the braes leading to the best points of view,' he wrote, 'and a marine garden, laid out with much taste in the sloping hollow of a sheltered glen, extends down to the very edge of the sea'. Designed by John Smith, the Aberdeen architect who planned the reconstruction of Slains Castle in 1836/37, the villa was built in 1840 for George Hamilton-Gordon, fourth Earl of Aberdeen. Orphaned by the time he was twelve years old, the future Laird of Haddo was brought up by his guardians, Prime Minister William Pitt the Younger and Viscount Melville, the political 'Manager' of Scotland. Educated at Harrow and Cambridge, he became a special ambassador to Austria in 1813 and thereafter played a prominent role in European diplomacy and British politics before serving as Prime Minister from 1852 to 1855. The 'marine villa' became the Earl's Lodge Hotel, which, gutted by fire in 1984, was a ruin until restoration as a dwelling house began in 2005.

The Commissioners of the Northern Lighthouses were petitioned in 1819 and again in 1822 to build a lighthouse in the neighbourhood of Boddam. In 1824 they decided to act and purchased the islet known as the Yards of Boddam as a suitable site the following year. Built of local granite by Robert Stevenson, grandfather of the author R.L. Stevenson, the 118-feet-high Buchanness Lighthouse was operational in 1827, with a lantern (invented by the builder) that had a range of sixteen nautical miles. The king of the Netherlands presented Stevenson with a medal to honour his invention, which was later described as 'a flashing light, which in every five seconds of time emerges from a state of partial darkness, and exhibits a momentary light, resembling a star of first magnitude'. Dated September 1840, a report in the *New Statistical Account of Scotland* stated that the lighthouse 'has answered all the good purposes anticipated, both in regard to the shipping interest generally and those engaged in the herring industry at Peterhead and along the coast.' A foghorn, locally known as the 'Boddam Coo' (cow) because of its three blasts every ninety seconds, was installed in 1904. Previously, villagers beating tin basins with spoons alerted fogbound mariners to the hazards of the coast.

BODDAM FROM BUCHANNESS LIGHTHOUSE

Boddam was renowned for summer-dried haddocks and so, when he sold the site for Buchanness Lighthouse, the village superior, Bailie Robertson, reserved the right of the fisher families to spread fish to dry on the adjacent sand-free rocks. He also confirmed their right to beach boats in the channel between the Yards of Boddam and the mainland. Note the boat beached on the right, northward of the far end of the bridge. In 1840 this channel was described as 'a south and north boat harbour, the latter being also capable of receiving ships of moderate draught of water'. It was claimed that 'a most commodious little harbour', with an entry from the south and the north and 'a greater depth of water than in the present harbours of Peterhead', could be made at a cost of £1,500 to £1,800. In 1845 the fourth Earl of Aberdeen spent over £2,000 on building a pier in the channel on the northern side of the bridge and then arranged for Boddam to be registered as a port. Remnants of the pier and of a guiding light for the north entrance to the 'harbour' can still be seen.

Boddam

The cottages clustered on both sides of the road leading from the landward end of the bridge pictured on the previous page illustrate how dwellings in the old seatown of Boddam were sited haphazardly. This, the oldest part of the village, was designated E when the first steps were taken to name streets in Boddam. After the village superior, Bailie Robertson, advertised for settlers to occupy a planned extension to the seatown in May 1824, new streets were laid out on the north and west of the original village. In 1794 the population of the seatown was 192. Including residents in the lighthouse complex and those in houses on the outskirts of the village proper, the 1871 census numbered 803 inhabitants. No streets were named and houses in the village were numbered consecutively from 1 to 132. By 1874/75, A, B, C, D and E Streets had been named as such. The herring nets draped out to dry on the dike at the junction of B and C Streets indicate that the scene was probably photographed at the end of the summer herring fishing season when the nets were taken home to be repaired.

C. STREET, BODDAM

Looking seaward along C Street, Buchanness Lighthouse stands clear above the rooftops. Less obvious, the foghorn – the 'Boddam Coo' – can be seen above the rooftop directly beyond the motorbus. Identification of streets by letters continued until 1955/56. Thereafter, B became Gordon Street; D – Russell Street; E – Earl's Court; and N – New Street. The renaming of A and C Streets was less straightforward. Some of the addresses on A became part of Rocksley Drive and, roughly speaking, the rest of A became the 'bottom' part of Queen's Road with C as the 'top' part.

The 'harbour' created in 1845 by the Earl of Aberdeen became outdated by developments in the herring fishery. Bigger drifters required deeper harbours with quays suitable for handling the larger catches. In 1857, of sixty-two Boddam-owned herring boats, twenty-four fished from the village; the others worked from Peterhead. Some of Boddam's inadequacies were remedied temporarily after the new village superior, William Aiton – a sub-contractor who helped to build the Suez Canal – constructed a new harbour; in 1878, seventy-eight drifters were landing herrings for curers in Boddam. The deficiencies of the harbour, however, were progressively exposed. By 1905 many sailing drifters working from the main ports measured over sixty-five feet; none of the thirty-four boats based in Boddam were over fifty feet. The advent of the steam drifter sounded the death knell of Boddam as a port of any significance and, in the late 1920s, one visitor found 'grass growing on the piers', a 'few small-line boats in the harbour', and 'old men earning a living catching lobsters and crabs'.

The number of quarries in the Boddam area increased as a result of the Industrial Revolution. In addition, 'Peterhead' granite, produced in quarries at Stirling Hill and Blackhill, gained a worldwide reputation for decorative and monumental purposes. It was used, for example, in the Stock Exchange, Foreign Office, and Covent Garden in London; the Royal Exchange, Bradford; and the Union Bank, Glasgow. Pedestals of 'Peterhead' granite were used for Sir Francis Drake's statue in Plymouth; the Duke of Wellington's statue in front of Buckingham Palace; and for a memorial in Vilna to the Russian Empress Catherine II. Over twenty quarries were working during the boom years. As a result of European competition, only seven remained operational in 1905. One of them, opened at Stirling Hill in the 1880s to supply granite for the breakwaters for the Harbour of Refuge at Peterhead, was worked by convicts housed in a specially built prison on the outskirts of Peterhead. A purpose-built standard gauge railway, about 2? miles long, linked the quarry to a work yard in the prison and also to a harbour created in the bay for barges used in the project. The final granite block was laid on the north breakwater on 27 September 1956. Blackhill Quarry, pictured here, belonged to a company founded by Heslop and Wilson in 1858. By 1950 it was the last commercial quarry in the area, but was closed soon afterwards along with the company's polishing works at Boddam.

Boddam

High Street, Buchanhaven

Wishing you a Happy New Year.

In December 1812 James Ferguson of Pitfour, the proprietor of the lands of Blackhouse on the northern outskirts of Peterhead, advertised in the *Aberdeen Journal* that he intended to develop the village of Buchanhaven where there were 'houses already to accommodate three boats' hands'. With various kinds of bait readily accessible and 'a good landing place', he emphasised the potential of the village as a base for white fishing and 'was desirous that proper persons in this line come forward and settle there'. Photographed nearly a century later, this scene gives graphic confirmation of the realisation of the laird's plans. High Street, with typical fishermen's cottages stretching its whole length, is fringed with baskets of 'sma'lins'. The family in the foreground, engaged in preparing lines for the next day's fishing, obviously saw nothing incongruous in their workplace encroaching on the main street. They were, after all, replicating a scene familiar in the fishing villages throughout Buchan.

A FISHER SCENE AT BUCKHAVEN. PETERHEAD.   93708.

This scene was photographed in Buchanhaven, not Buckhaven as printed on the caption. Most of the fishermen in Buchanhaven participated in the annual summer herring fishery in the North Sea. The custom of extended family ownership of boats persisted in spite of rising costs – from £100-£120 for a boat and gear in the 1840s to £300-£400 by 1890. A big rise in the requisite capital investment, caused by the advent of the steam drifter, led to non-family members – e.g. fish salesmen, ship chandlers, coal merchants – taking shares in boats. In the seasonal 'settle up', profits were divided on an agreed ratio basis between boat owners, net owners and 'hired men' – crew members with no monetary investment in boat or gear. During the season, crews carried out running repairs to nets aboard the boats; at the end of the season, net owners overhauled their own gear at home. This was often done in the open air. Women helped by mending holes in the mesh, but, as shown here, men usually undertook the replacement of other parts, such as 'ozzels' – short cords tying the mesh to the head-rope. Note the ad hoc arrangement of hanging the net from a hook driven into the wall of the cottage while the other end was attached to the handle of the door.